pictureshowpress.net

FIRST EDITION

ISBN-13: 978-1-7341702-1-4

daughter of salt

poetry by
chestina craig

picture show press

Poems

daughter of summer sweat

daughter of easy tears

daughter of the pacific

daughter of summer sweat

coven

I govern the change in my life by
summers, everything relative to the months
my skin doesn't stand on-end
vacation sun sheltering
my childhood coven,
us barefoot-baby-witches,
the magic all in how we drag
our feet on the asphalt & do not bleed
the magic in how we race the boys
downhill & always win.
rule out of a plastic castle
sourgrass—our hemlock death flower
mix a potion of innocence, sleepover silence
the poison we pick, that is something
other than girlhood
something other than being shameful,
dirty or mean, the way the TV told us,
fresh sweat & strawberries shared like secrets
we pluck the gravel out of each other's knees
& ride on, the day is ending
but there is so much light to cast
our bodies into
& so much
summer left
for us.

summer prom

after SZA, for Rhea

it is August
& 'Prom' by SZA plays through Rhea's car stereo
the loudest I've ever heard it.
prom is to *promenade* & that is what we do
through the streets of La Jolla,
our teeth chime loud,
crystal champagne glasses along to the song.
it is late afternoon, but we are morning glory,
blooming violet, so purple
I could swallow it.

we are so beautiful only the music can hold us,
& isn't this a tiny revolution?
to pick what we will allow to be
boat or blanket for our bodies?

this summer is omnipresent
everything tangerine juice blurred.
summer is to *half year*,
is to *pack horse* in Latin.
this warm animal carries us
to our own good ocean.

I watch Rhea sing a song
that also becomes a high-rise in her mouth
& prom sounds like *promise*

& today I vow
to build more churches
for times like this.

ode to Mr. Brightside

after the killers

ode to this childhood anthem,
the only cage I ever freed myself from
my teen heart lock picked open,
the only time I can sing
"doin' just fine" & not bleed
some false hope.
these words just a mouthful of gold
I forget my friends & I don't own for once,
something we will sell out of
before the night is done or the car
stops, but right now
everything glitters & it's ours
every light in the room orbits
us like a sunrise.
destiny calls us dancing,
& opens our eyes to see
that the bright
side of our bodies
is every single one.

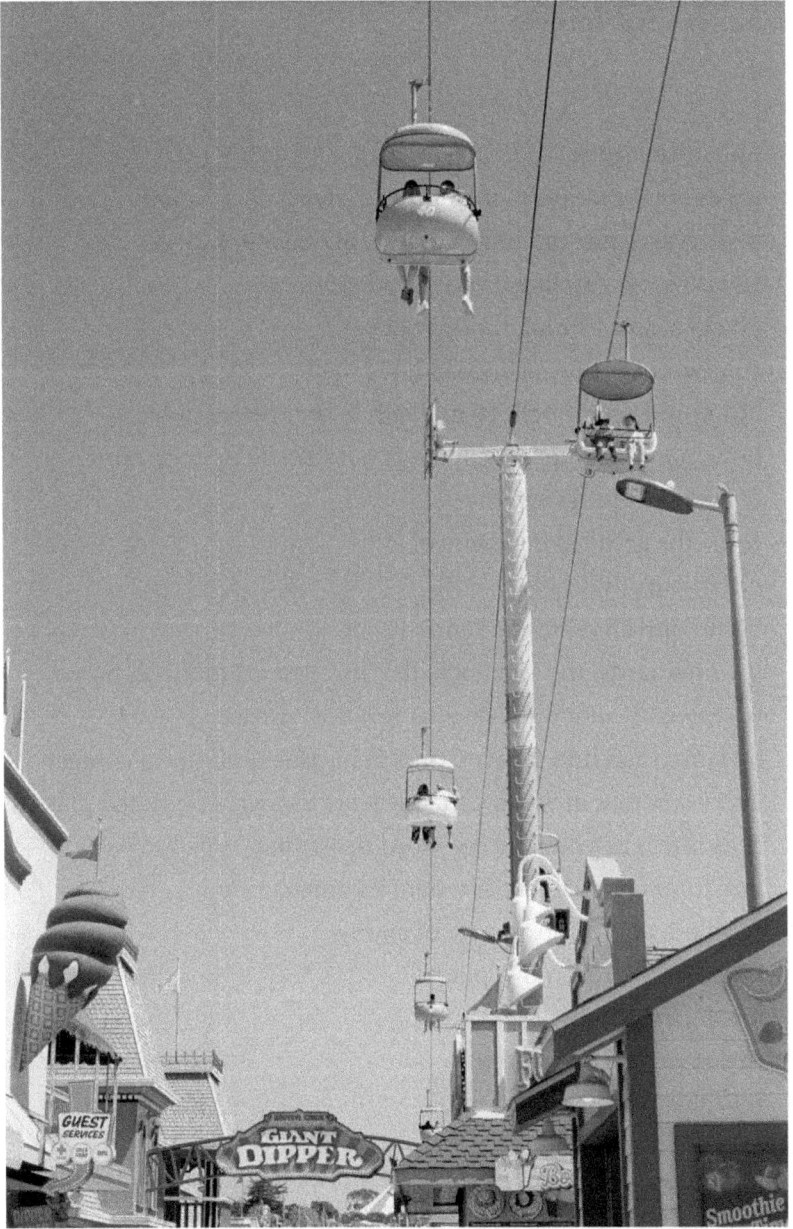

Santa Cruz forever

I blame every Santa Cruz summer
for every ounce of invincibility I've felt,
if you can come out of the thaw still deer spry,
swallow the sun like those born here,
you can do anything underwater
& how many times should I have died
but at 16 I didn't believe in death & so it never came,
how many scientists wish they could bottle up teen faith
& feed it to believers
& us, the greatest believers of all
not in ourselves,
but in ourselves all the same
the lifeguards, the surf rock, the unrolled windows & how
we knew it all would save us & it did, sunset
by sunset tan line, by new pink skin peeled off like a contest
every summer in Santa Cruz presents its own rose-tinted glasses,
& as much as you love the word drowning
you forget its realness & where it comes from
& where you come from & of course
it has always been this place
this burnt beach
this grain of glassy sand
this heat transfer
of course you begin & end here
what other existence is there,
to be swallowed whole by the sounds
of young girls discovering their own
kind of immortality.

tough bitch

tough bitch doesn't like shoes
will get a whole plant stuck in her foot before she gives in,
says I already have everything I need to walk on the bottom of
    my feet.
tough bitch loves callouses
loves tan lines, bruises
the way harshness changes the skin for the stronger
loves to watch the give of a body
wears scars like a new gold

tough bitch keeps two hammers under her pillow
will be damned if you ever catch her unprepared
catch her naked of weapons
was upset the year her brother got a pocket knife for Christmas
& she didn't
bought one for herself the next day

came out of her first cathedral swimming
has never been afraid of the ocean
will break a grin at a 10ft swell
cracked out a baby tooth sharply on a surf board
and never fished it back from the sea
can imagine all the softness it's given up by living there

tough bitch is always the only girl on the boat
but least afraid to cradle the fish
least afraid of a hook in the jaw

always most ready to hit a wave and buck over the sides
like something feral
like tough bitch going home

tough bitch can put on a whole set of snow chains by herself
while her boyfriend watches from the car
tough bitch will do the hard things
& this is so much of the way she knows love
to resurface from the under tow
bruised, joyed in the blood
& still say, "that was so much fun."

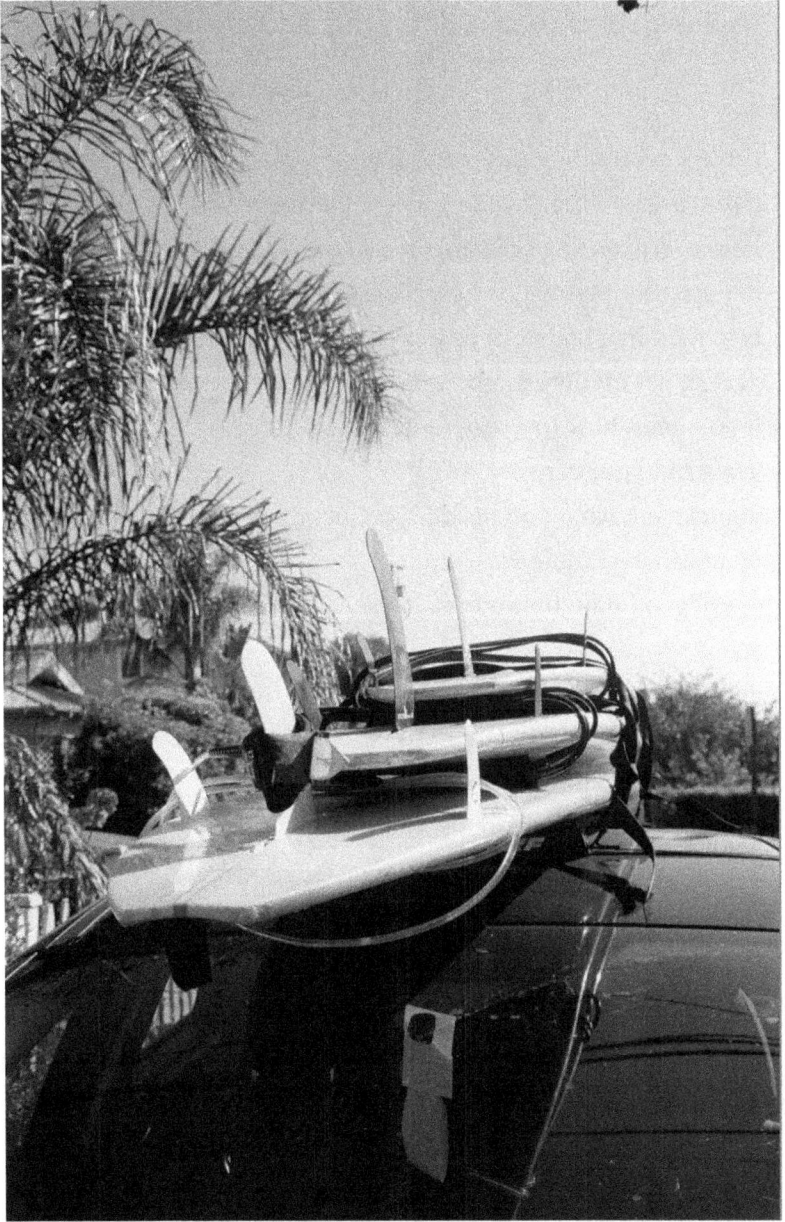

restlessness as trauma or coping mechanism

get up, get up they can't ignore you
if you are moving, swallowed gold like seafish,
I am every darting scale my body loses to the light
get up, get up you look best blurry
best with half body on the next frame
get up, get up they might just love you
if you learn how to dance, quarter slip
grace out your ear.
you can get what you need if you just melt
& mold, like candle wax, child,
every good daughter burns.

get up, get up he cannot find you if you slip
into school like a lost letter,
paper in the wind, if you
silver sliver sardine run like the rest,
hide in your wide hands like the visible sky.
get up, get up the beasts & their noses are coming,
& your feet are calloused & bare,
your legs know invisibility like tripwire,
like looking for the camouflage in a girl,
get up, get up, he can't gaslight
if you are already smoke
constantly vibrating like a sound wave,
get up, get up I am pulsing
in no defined location.
let the road take me,

sun off the tide: lost light.
search for me,
but do not find a thing.

Santa Catalina is thirsty

I am living on an island
in its worst drought in history,
even the cactus are dying.
It sits on top of saltwater
it cannot use.
I too know what it is like
to have what you need beneath you,
& not be able to drink.

daughter of easy tears

a poem in which I cannot hide from my flaws so I name them publicly

I am such a hungry thing, the seventh sin,
all baby bird but just its mouth, wide open & endless
don't you know how much I can stomach & want for more
don't you know about the sinking swamps, the fires how they
    consume
have you ever seen my hands not holding
onto something, white-knuckled & cracking
like an infant, I forget my own strength
like an infant, I am desperate for anything

like an undertaker, I bury everything in me that does not shine
& leave it in the backyard to rot
you will not catch the smell until you get too close
like all damned fruit, I am only sweet in the summer
like all damned fruit, the trees will drop me soon enough

like any good tree I forget that light needs to hit the ground too
there are two sides to every shadow, the darkness
& the figure in the way
sometimes I am both

like any good tree I fear the fire,
even when I am that wild myself.
look at all the circles I can run around my body
I won't ever give them up
like any evergreen in the winter

I hold all the sap & sick like it birthed me,
I will not let any of this go,
even if I should
even if I wanted to.

portrait of the poet as her ex-lover's grin

the boy tells me he is injured hare,
willow swishing his broken bloody
below tender ground.
I follow him down the rabbit hole,
    & he salts the earth with my hair.
the boy cries wolf
    & I am high on saving him,
a fresh plate of fruit I place myself
unceremoniously in his mouth.
the boy survives on this body &
tells me I am most beautiful
                  while wilting
like every good plant in the winter,
it is a good game I play with myself,
how dead he can make me feel.

in a dream, I chewed my way free
from the borough to swallow any light,
but all I know is the beast he raised
from the dead.
I ask for a shovel to dig us out
& he calls me fox, sly bitch,
says I am trying to trade him for the sun.

the boy cries wolf, his mouth white as the moon
& now I know the thing he has been
all along.

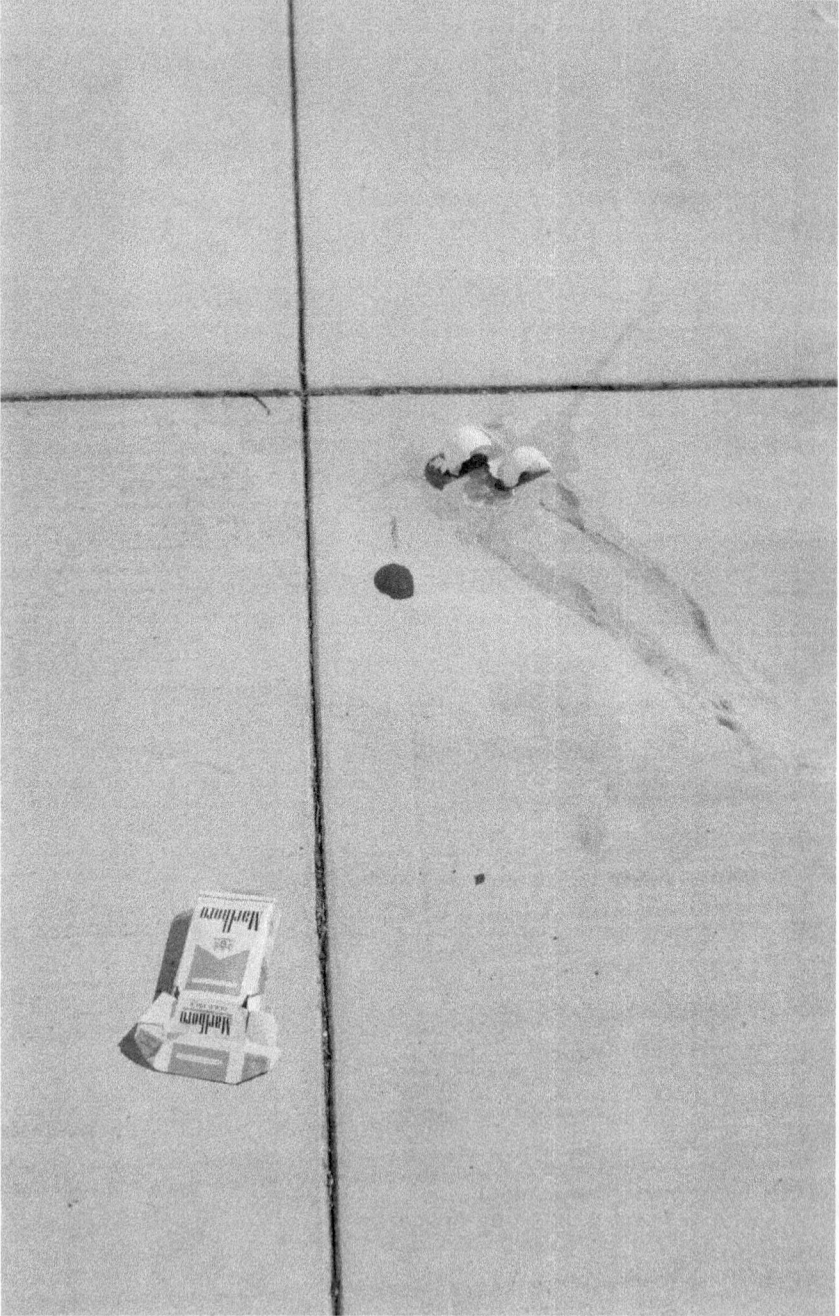

alternative universe where my Grandmother does not burn to death in Her kitchen cooking breakfast for a man

after Olivia Gatwood

alternative universe where my Grandma
sleeps in for a change, wallows
in bed like the youth
She gave up.
She does not cook
my grandpa breakfast today,
does not wear a flammable coffin, instead
She stays alive in silk & smokes
my grandpa's cigarettes on the porch & lets him
yell himself hoarse & blows smoke
into the kitchen that is not Her scorched body,
that is not the fire bridging a gap between food & disaster,
not the gas burner stretching its arms onto her skin
if death has ever been a warm embrace, it happens here
in the hospital burn unit
but no

today, my Grandmother calls my mom long distance,
& says, "honey, I'm so sorry."
She does not become salem catching up with my family,
keeps the heirloom of being a witch that refuses to swing.
if fire is a magical bounty hunter,
the women in my family are on the run
& in this world, my Grandma makes the marathon,
carries us safely across the finish line to water.

alternative universe where my Grandmother is alive.

& in this universe my Grandma is proud of me & my mom is
    proud of me
because she learns how to be
this time & this time,
my mother has a Mother who can hold her hand
through the cancer treatment, a sharp light
casting our faces less flattering
than a stove-top fire, a sacrifice,
even in this universe we are not safer.
we are still Women in every kind of lighting
still Witches on the flames
& the sickness on my mother's skin
looks just like burn marks.

once I broke my arm on my fourth grade mission field trip

my mom was a catholic but it's never quite left her bones,
you can see it when her eyes lift to the sky,
the conversations she has with her dead mother
everything that has heaved me
out its open mouth has been a witch,
the woman that made me can see

my mother prays like a crooked hand
reaching behind her back,
only can recall the saint of lost things,
which is why I take not being found
so personally

my father always makes sure I have flares in my car,
& my mother gives me a keychain blessed by the pope,
& when the metal back of my vehicle
caved in like the bay I love
I did not firework into the sky,
but I did live
& all of my bones a magic porcelain
unbroken

god is with you

after Melissa Lozada-Oliva

in Irish, we greet each other with *dia duit*
which directly translates to *god is with you*
in Irish, we greet each other over holy water saliva.
my Irish is a meager grain of sand,
a mouth begging for water,
the salton sea my body
cannot sink within.
*le do thoil** out my mouth like confession
more holy than hello.
more holy home than classroom,
my teeth are returning
to this old church

my great grandfather's Irish
grew cypress trees,
leaning like axon after the stroke,
still a holdfast in the storm on his tongue.
his Irish, the family blood clot.
my Irish, heart murmur misfiring
like a caged canary in my chest.
our Irish still living bone,
I lick clean.

please

pigeon point lighthouse

for St. Anthony, patron saint of lost things

it begins to rain & this is something I am never dressed for / is
not where I get my water / the peeling phone booth was
already a ghost / two years ago & I keep coming back to visit /
always bringing someone new / look at the lighthouse / look at
how we got here / something invisible pointed up the road &
we thought it was our idea / someone placed a prayer candle
by the phone & my brain said, *make this yours* / St. Anthony
made it ring from heaven / to remind me to keep looking / I am
still learning how to pray the right way / still learning how to
make smoke / some god tried to shake the sky's pockets & we
called it inconvenience / someone thought longer about the
most beautiful way to sign for help & I am jealous / I think my
mother was here / it is just a phone booth / I am just a light
house / invisible / pointing my fingers at the sky / asking
somebody to trust me / to follow my light / *I was lost, but now I
am found.*

addendum to tough bitch

I am a tough bitch because my father
is a soft man
I do not fear the dark or ocean
because he loves them,
used to take me on hikes
in the night, let my pupils dilate
let me know my body was made
for the science of this
always left the flashlights at home
& let me firefly, let me finish
all my sentences.
my father taught me to fish,
taught me to fight off fear with physics
& flew me home on a bike before I could ride
tweezed out every seed of summer
asphalt from my knees my whole 6th year,
my father let me hold a hammer first
know the comfort of its weight in my palms
& then make that heavy build a bookshelf,
gave me pocket knives & showed me the best ways
to shave a branch & all the arteries in my thigh
to cut away from, only to slice at things
that do not bleed.
my father taught me to swim,
took me out to the deepest water we could get to
& made me try to touch the bottom
& after every ragdoll of my body he showed me

how to resurface
how to stiffen in again, how to bite
back & laugh.

salt hum ii

if tears & sweat have the same ingredients, do our bodies force
us to weep when we ask the most of them?

daughter of the pacific

good salt

the ocean's love language is gift giving
which means every time you swim to shore
alive, is a present
every time you are more survived than the previous version
of yourself,
you should remove the wrapping paper
peel off the bikini in front of the mirror
such is summer citrus, always showing
where the sun & salt have touched you
better than a bruise, the ocean

swallows all broken glass,
the youthful liquor bottles,
takes in the thrown picture frame,
the unlucky mirror getting what it deserves,
my happy clumsy hands on a wine glass,
& gives them back soft,
now something that was never ours
which is to say, the ocean's love language is also acts of service
to turn a knife into decoration,

how long will it take to unmake me sharp
a making begging to melt, become touchable
how many baptisms must I take before I am good salt?
before I am worthy of decoration too.
I once called the ocean "something that takes so much"
& I've never sounded
so much like an ungrateful daughter.

portrait of the only woman on a boat

the fishermen are
mostly men,
I am authority figure but not
in charge but mostly
just a figure.
the fishermen
watch me
get dirty with a blood that is not my own
watch me wipe
my hands on my pants
a sticky-fingered child coated
in rotting death
the fishermen hand me towels,
are kind, want me
clean & smiling.
have me crawl into the tiny
cabins of their boats
to fetch the animals,
say I fit
there the best
ask me if I am scared, while I hold
something dying in my hands
& learn about it
I say no.
I don't always say no.
sometimes, I pin the fish as they thrash
which is to say, "I will not

be easy for you,"
hoist their heavy
beasts up while they
watch me
grow taller. watch me
like the swimmer that I am,
unhookable.
the fishermen want to take me on their boats,
ask me when I will work
for them. tell me they hunt
mermaids. tell me they do this
all the time, catch all the best ones.
a hunter is always a hunter
& I look like something the ocean held, slimy with salt
& the mouth I use to protect myself, the fishermen
look at me
like an animal
& they are not wrong.

to the parts of you that are Stevie Nicks at sunrise

after Farah Billah

I know you, wind woman
siren on the rocks in a white dress
watch what crashes into the rocks,
like glitter, scattering
all of you draped in sunset pink
& macramé & restlessness.

I know you witch,
the way you twirl as if
all that longing might fall off you
& cobweb into fringe, cast off
like a coat in the summer.

I see your heart beating too fast
for the church hall of your throat,
I see you swelling on stage,
the light must fill you somewhere
to come violent out your teeth
like that.

I know you woman.
they're playing your song.

marine biologist hands

are oddly dry for all the water they are steeped in,
pick scales off like dead skin
& begin to wonder if they too, are sprouting in the body
like fingernails that carry
so much salt in the crease of them,
looking for a sign that we have not stolen too much blue
that we have not danced more destructive than the tide,
all of our work is trying to hold this &
how can you lifeguard the ocean
when she is forced to drown in her own
empty waters.
harvested with a lead foot,
unspoken by the mouth of every whale supposed to outlive us.

us with the cracked hands trying to spoon
this water to safety, trying to feed the creatures,
but the ocean—the ocean *persists*,
she does not care about landmass borders or men or lies or science
no.
all the ocean cares about is birth
& having area to stretch into
& even as we take so much the ocean is expanding
& isn't it beautiful that something so threatened decides to be
    more space
& isn't that the best fight
to be more water
than your destroyer asked for.

in which I come close to explaining what the water means to me

a man tells me to stop writing poems about water
& the ocean & again a woman is asked to forget
what has a saved her.
& again no one ever asked him
to drop his writing about the feminine
& god, which really are the same thing.
a man asks me to forget what has saved me
& again I go back,
to high school & the pool
& the fact that ghosts are afraid of water
& my lover who haunted me,
when the only place I was safe
& unreachable was under the surface,
where his voice could not carry,
where his phantom arms
would dissolve if they reached for me,
such a fan of how I could be miles away
& still belong to him
such a fan of my strings,
loose & ripped out all caught up in the wind
how he could twist
til they looked like his words.
& the ocean has always held me
like I owed it nothing

but I should not write about the water
because a man is afraid
of how much I love myself now,
is afraid of the ways something so vast
can chose me back.
& again my sadness is not tortured enough
to be digestible for him
thinks I owe him my gore,
a man thinks my gore is not
bones enough for him,
thinks the way I've pushed past my emotional abuse
is cliché,
writes a friend-zone poem in its place.

I think about the time I was cheated on,
unallowed to sink my nails into anger,
& hold it like it existed.
I remember being turned against my mother,
my friends,
I remember all backs against mine but the waters.
I remember the hole he dug,
I remember him handing me the shovel & telling me,
it was in my hands the whole time.
I remember the water,

I remember the water,
when I left him, I leaped off a high dive
& again my body hitting the water
wasn't muse enough,
but I don't care about that,

I care about being feral,
being survived.
I care about where I hide from the ghost of his voice.
my recovery like swimming,
I use every muscle under this skin
to keep my body at the surface,
determined not to strand
like a lost captain.

a man tells me to stop writing about the ocean
& he forgets where I have been,
what I have waded through to get here,
forgets his manners,
forgets that the ocean
& my resilience are stretched enough for all poems.
I am seastar, ripped limb from limb,
always growing back,
replacing what I have lost.
you can ask me to stop writing poems
about the water,
but I will never forget
what saved me.

Athena

*for the 14ft Hammerhead Shark caught off a beach in Texas
that died after it was brought to shore*

where I've been, great hammerheads are named after Gods,
this is the best way to recognize what they were before land existed.

somewhere in the south of this magnolia tree country,
along miles of the Atlantic ocean's extended tongue,

a man hooks Athena on his line & thinks himself god,
a child shaking a bee in a bottle,

pulls the shark ashore & straddles her like hell's horseman,
jerks her head up to the camera & demands a smile. all teeth.

later when they interview him, the news clamoring
at his deadly door, he mourns like a good man

insists like a church preacher how he tried
to teach her to swim. benevolent god

to the bone. & Athena & I remember
every hook we've ever felt through our skin

every reverse drowning & the landlocked hands
crossing themselves up & down like forgiveness we will not bestow

she was a beast that wasn't supposed to die, which goes to show,
they never thought her alive in the first place.

hunger

for Ruby & Bimini
after Florence & The Machine

& I feel fullest barefoot drunk
with my feet off the ground
& it's so beautiful that we left our sandals
by the door & we still feel invincible
enough to sway our way home,
to a place where none of us are related
but still share the same blood,
step squarely on rocks & still
keep our skin unopened,
this is a force

& we shake like we have an army of birds to lead
like there is feather in our bones
hollowed out to hold,
the ways we've been holding each other

& we're so full that we left the bar for the stars,
like they were waiting for us,
& turn them all the way up,
I hold one between us
that plays this song—a new beast into our bodies

if there is such a thing as a good possession
it happens now,
we're filled up with the waves,

we are falling away,
shaken down this dirt road & our family
says we look like fireflies
like summer's sister,
like night breath & this
is all I've ever wanted to be
a warm season's glow in the dark
& a song stuck on repeat.

ode to Ches-tee-nuh

ode to this name my father gave me,
borrowed from great aunt, never married,
New Jersey woman, Chestina on her own
Chestina raised her sisters,
so much gardener in this name already

ode to middle school
the cruelty of children trapped by youth & wanting.
they alchemy the shame out of something that is mine,
they hack my name into different sections
& make it into another word for my body parts,
the boys make it a reminder about all the ways
my figure is just an animal falling short
rearrange the letters to spell out slaughterhouse.
these days I cut my label off at the neck
ask you to call me ches
ask you to let me bud alone

ode to my mother's hand around my tiny hand,
her chin up to the department store women,
pointing fingers:
"you named her that with breasts like that?"
ode to my mother's double D's
ode to everything my mother has carried
shoulders like an everyday incantation
a woman's DNA does not get that daring for nothing

ode to my fourteen-year-old clenched jaw
in the face of adult men,
their sneers,
eyes on the skin over my murmuring blood
the place where it becomes hot in the body.
their asking me to live up to my name,
is a gross prayer over a teen girl

ode to the ways I have stretched into this
for myself.
the fruit I am growing, my body
an orchard, sunlight & soil.
I can fill your stomachs
& will always grow back, stronger

ode to *my* name,
all the times you've called me Christina
& I let you.
this tiny battle I never pick.
ode to the frat boys who always tried to wrap
their tongue around my epithet,
but got lost, halfway through
my name is party trick,
your favorite joke tacked onto this body
but I am not the assistant,
instead I am the magician casting the spell.
my name is magic, a declaration,
blank slate, its own pantheon
my name has no ghost stories
to swallow it,

no baby book to tell you
so I define it myself

Chestina—ashes
Chestina—ocean
Chestina—gold
Chestina, the daughter, the named
ode to the beauty when you get it right
the syllables curving like a mountain climb
the break, the springboard end
ode to my title
ode to the first thing I ever owned.

when you think of me, just imagine me in the ocean saying "more light"

after Lyd Havens

more light / & by more light I mean more waking & stirring
with a window wide open to hope / & more songs that feel like
a beast of violins swelling in your belly / & by violins I mean
birds in the morning/ & by morning I mean letting the light
share time with grief / more looking in the mirror & only seeing
a photo of you doing something you love / when I say more
light I mean more lemons just as they are / more of that yellow /
more claiming it in your smile / more zest to carry along with
you / when I say zest I mean your feet leave the ground with
music often / more juice / more sugar / more salt / more ocean /
more flinging your body into it with the knowledge of
numbness / more refusing to be chained to home by the cold /
more remembering that you are the heat / the heaving of the
earth / more dancing like you have an army of animals to lead /
like you were raised barefoot / more calloused feet / more
sleeping in new places / more stretching like a vine on its way
to the sky / by stretching I mean bending like you have only
ever known good hands / more surface area open to the sun /
by surface area I mean take up space / more blood rush / more
hummingbird dresses / more linen / more wings / more salt
before the swelling / by swelling I mean a feeling that builds
like physics in the cathedral of your body / when I say your
body I mean more of that / more of your body / by body I mean
light / more light / more of you / & the ways light moves
around your shape that exists / so bright.

sharks are for girls

sharks are for girls, who else than those with tough skin
& a body of teeth
who else than 400 million years
of evolution smart, older than trees & dirt,
who else than these daughters of salt,
the way we swim continuously, are born doing it
through pink & lace frosting & men telling us about ourselves,
watch how we breathe by doing almost anything,
watch how we hold the ocean together with needle, mouth &
    thread,
everything less healthy without us in the math,
watch how we bear our teeth & smile,
how we are punished blood trophy

who knows more about blood than us?
knows more about metal & hunt than us?
how we have to prove we are worth more alive than dead?
girlhood & salt & sharks, we are the underestimated intelligence,
misunderstood villains, look how little it takes for us to be evil,
think us dumb man-eaters,
god bless our snaggle tooth,
each of our survival instincts

a group of sharks is sometimes called a shiver
therefore we can name a group of women a coven
a group of girls a quake,
a movement of the earth

& what better place for girls than the ocean
all mirror on the good days,
sunlit vanity,
show us our reflection, this battle cry
fuck myths
fuck mermaids
what better animal to keep for women than the shark?
have you ever seen them swim?
seen them feed?
seen them at the bathroom sink?
of course you sense death in a drop of water,
of course you go to the source
of course they think you're angry, they love you less that way

when they tell you to smile think of their jaws,
serrated teeth all for tearing & more than enough
to spare a few.

& when they bait you
don't forget to steal all of it
of course sharks are for girls,
the females always grow largest anyway.

Acknowledgements

thank you to all of the publications where previous versions of these poems were featured:

Anti-Heroin Chic ("restlessness as trauma or coping mechanism"); *Barren Magazine* ("Athena" and "good salt"); *Black Napkin Press* ("ode to Mr. Brightside" & "pigeon pt. lighthouse"); *Bombus Press* ("god is with you"); *Graviton Lit* ("marine biologist hands"); *Harness Magazine* ("when you think of me imagine me in the ocean saying 'more light'" & "for the parts of you that are Stevie Nicks at sunrise"); *Honey & Lime* ("a poem in which I cannot hide from my flaws so I name them publicly"); *L' Ephemerere Review* ("sharks are for girls" & "ode to ches-tee-nuh"); *Moon Child Magazine* ("summer prom" & "portrait of the poet as her ex lover's grin"); *Rising Phoenix Review* ("portrait as the only woman on the boat"); *Sea Foam Magazine* ("coven"); and *Vagabond City Lit* ("Santa Cruz forever").

Gratitude

First, I would like to thank Shannon Phillips for taking a chance
on my work, and for taking the utmost care in publishing
it. I appreciate it more than you will ever know.

Thank you to the Pacific Ocean for raising me & to the Atlantic
for always feeling like a childhood friend.

My grandmothers, for teaching me to take no shit.

My family, for reminding me that I can be anything.

Jay, for the past four plus years of love, for making me sit down
and get the book in perfect order & always reminding me
that it's going to be okay.

Farah, my angel, my best friend, thank you for making life feel
like magic.

Leigh, Megan & Zoe, for your unending support that I can feel
from all over the world.

Julia & Olivia, for surfing the Pacific with me, and for making
Santa Cruz home again.

Alison & Brooke, for your immense wisdom, for being so
absolutely powerful, but also kind.

Cole & Syd, for making me feel like no time has passed
between us ever, for your forever acceptance.

Word Church, for always being a home & a place that my work
is safe even in the beginning of its birth.

Bimini & my fellow interns, for the best two months of my life
& endless inspiration.

Wilton, for your undying love.

You, the reader, for handling my salt with love and care.

Chestina Craig grew up in Santa Cruz, California. She currently lives on the California Coast with her cat, Wilton. Her work has been published with *Crab Fat Magazine*, *Vagabond City Lit*, Button Poetry, and others. She has presented her writing at events such as The Young Women's Empowerment Conference, and open mics around the United States. As a holder of a bachelor's degree in marine biology, she was once friends with an octopus. She recently spent two months in the Bahamas at a field station assisting with shark and stingray research. At twenty five years old, she is excited to look into a hopeful future in marine biology, where she still finds enough time to write. She hopes that one day she will only be required to wear comfortable clothing, study the ocean, and get paid to have too many feelings. Her chapbook, "body of water," came out October 2017 with Sadie Girl Press. "daughter of salt" is her second chapbook publication. You can find more information at chestinacraig.com, Instagram, and Twitter: @chesseaa

www.ingramcontent.com/pod-product-compliance
Lightning Source LLC
Chambersburg PA
CBHW071932020426
42331CB00010B/2833